From Space to the Seabed

THE GREAT ADVENTURES SERIES
From Space to the Seabed

Jonathan Rawlinson

Rourke Enterprises, Inc.
Vero Beach, Florida 32964

Controlled by complex and specially developed equipment, undersea habitats prove man can live for long periods on the seabed.

LIBRARY OF CONGRESS
Library of Congress Cataloging-in-Publication Data

Rawlinson, Jonathan, 1944-
 From space to the seabed / by Jonathan Rawlinson.

  p. cm. — (Great adventure series)
 Includes index.
 Summary: Describes the United States Navy's experimental project, Sealab, in which divers lived and worked in an underwater habitat. Focuses on the experiences of astronaut Scott Carpenter who served on the crew of Sealab II.
 ISBN 0-86592-872-X
 1. Project Sealab — Juvenile literature. [1. Project Sealab. 2. Carpenter, M. Scott (Malcolm Scott), 1925-   .] I. Title. II. Series.
GC66.R38 1988
910 '09146 - dc19   88-15815
                              CIP
                               AC

CONTENTS

A Journey into Space

On April 9, 1959, the National Aeronautics and Space Adminstration [NASA] held a press conference in Washington, D.C. The space agency had been formed only six months earlier, and they were announcing the names of the first seven astronauts. The selection process been long. From several hundred applicants, 18 men had been selected as semi-finalists, and six were to have been chosen to train as astronauts. But NASA found it impossible to decide among seven of those men, so all seven were named as astronauts for Project Mercury, America's first manned space project. Among the seven was Navy Lieutenant Malcolm Scott Carpenter. He would become the second American to orbit the earth.

Malcolm Scott Carpenter was born on May 1, 1925 in Boulder, Colorado. He entered Colorado College in 1943 and then attended the University of Colorado. Carpenter loved flying and he joined the Navy for flight training in 1949. After serving in the Korean War from 1950 to 1953 on anti-submarine patrols, he joined the Navy Test Pilot School at Patuxent River, Maryland. It was only natural that when

Mercury was to be launched by an Atlas rocket from a launch pad at Cape Canaveral, Florida.

Malcolm Scott Carpenter was one of seven astronauts selected by NASA in 1959 to fly the one-man Mercury space capsule.

Project Mercury came along he should be chosen as one of its astronauts.

The first Mercury flight took place on May 5, 1961, when Alan Shepard shot into space on an up-and-down flight lasting just over 15-minutes. He was followed in July that year by Virgil Grissom. On February 20, 1962, John Glenn was put into space for three **orbits** of the earth, which lasted just under five hours. Then it was Carpenter's turn in a capsule he named *Aurora 7*. "I think of Project Mercury and the open manner in which we are conducting it for the benefit of all mankind as a light in the sky," he explained. "Aurora also means the dawn of a new age."

Carpenter thundered into orbit from the launch pad at Cape Canaveral on May 24, 1962. It was early morning, and within a few minutes the astronaut was weightless in space. He noticed that the sky quickly changed from blue to black, and very soon he was traveling into night on the dark side of the earth. At one point he sent a greeting to listeners on the ground as he passed over Mexico. "Hola, amigos, felicitaciónes a Mexico y especialmente a mis amigos de

After launch, Carpenter's mission was tracked by engineers in a special control center at Cape Canaveral.

8

Guyamas" ["Hello, friends, greetings to Mexico and especially to my friends of Guyamas"].

He orbited the earth three times, and then his tiny capsule came hurtling back to earth. From a speed of approximately 17,500 MPH the capsule was slowed by friction with the air. This heated the skin of the Mercury capsule until it glowed red. Inside, Carpenter could do nothing but sit and listen as the loud hiss became a distant roar and then a loud rumble. The **heat shield** at the base of the capsule prevented it from burning up. Carpenter was lying with his back against the shield only a couple of feet away from 3,500 degrees!

As planned, *Aurora 7* splashed down in the Atlantic Ocean, but far from where it was supposed to be. Carpenter scrambled out of his capsule and into a tiny life raft, where he waited to be rescued. Help came when helicopters arrived and dropped swimmers into the sea, but it was three hours before he was safely on the deck of the USS *Intrepid.* Carpenter's one and only space flight was over, but he was already looking forward to a new challenge, which was to carry him to the depths of the ocean.

Mercury capsules splashed down in the water and their astronauts were recovered and taken back to shore.

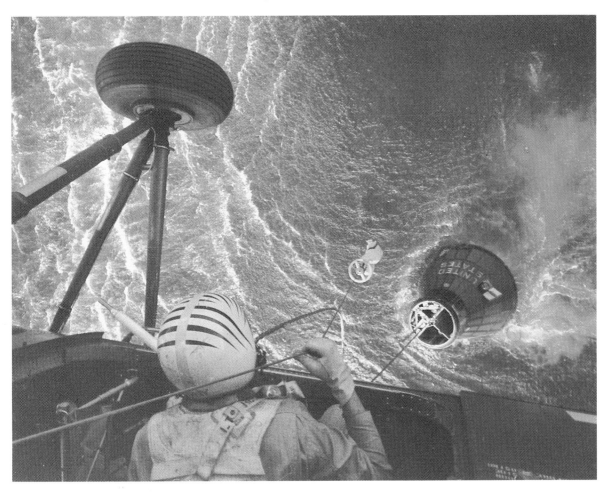

To the Ocean Floor

When Carpenter returned from space he knew he had helped open a new frontier. Many astronauts would follow his trail into space, and some would reach the moon. In 1962, the possibility of a moon landing seemed like a long way off. NASA was building a two-man spacecraft for tests around the earth. Before sending Apollo astronauts to the moon, NASA had been challenged by President Kennedy in May 1961 to land two men on the surface of the moon by the end of that decade. So far, no U.S. astronaut had been in space longer then five hours. For moon missions the astronauts would have to remain in space for about two weeks.

NASA was interested in seeing how people stood up to long periods away from home in strange situations. They studied submarine crews to see how they coped with being underwater for several days. They looked at scientific expeditions living in danger on ice floes in the Antarctic. Anything that helped NASA understand how to pick astronauts for long-duration flight was important.

President Kennedy had called space a "new ocean," and to one astronaut, the sea and space were closely linked. Both could be explored by people, but only under special conditions with protective clothing, a safe place to live, and proper safety measures. Both sea and space seemed to offer a lot. They were both unexplored

Remotely Operated Vehicles (ROVs) allow scientists to explore the floor of the ocean without having to send men to dangerous depths.

territory, places to test new scientific equipment, and areas where new resources might be found. To Malcolm Scott Carpenter it was natural to want to find out if people could live in space and under the sea.

In the early 1960s, many people were concerned about the fast population growth on the planet. Human beings would surely need more space on earth. Could the oceans be harvested for food? Would the seabed provide access to new minerals? Were there reasons for people to live and work at the bottom of the sea to make all these

Called Duplus, this ROV can carry either a load of scientific instruments or a small transparent cabin for the deep-sea explorer.

things happen? Many thought there were. Some scientists had even tried to develop **underwater habitats**, places where scientists and engineers ccould live and work for weeks on end.

In 1942 Jacques Cousteau and his friend Emile Gagnan, both from France, invented the means by which divers could carry air down beneath the surface and swim with an air line. It was called **scuba**, for self-contained underwater breathing apparatus. Scuba gear consisted of an air tank, a mouthpiece, and a hose connecting the two. The mouthpiece was designed to control the amount of air the diver inhaled. As the diver exhaled, the used air, mostly poisonous carbon dioxide gas, went directly into the water, forming little bubbles. Next, scientists wanted to see if people could live in underwater habitats.

Between 1957 and 1963, Captain George F. Bond of the U.S. Navy carried out many experiments with rats, goats, monkeys, and human beings to watch their behavior while breathing different mixtures of air and other gases. Bond wanted to see if the world's oceans could be used to provide animal protein for food. Called Genesis, Bond's project laid the groundwork for exciting research using people living at the bottom of the sea. Genesis was selected as the name for the experiments because they were a step leading to "dominion over the sea," as promised in Genesis, the first book of the Bible. By the early 1960s, the U.S. Navy was ready for the first real step toward making that dream a reality.

Developed by the Navy, this transparent bubble acts like a cocoon protecting the diver as he explores underwater.

Detached from the main ROV mother-ship, this small robot called Sprint is used to explore wrecks and underwater structures.

13

Sealab

There are many dangers for people wanting to explore deep beneath the surface of the sea. Most of them come from the fact that the pressure of water increases the deeper the diver goes. Water cannot be compressed, but the pressure it exerts deep down can squeeze air surrounding a diver until it enters body tissue. Deep water is also very cold and can injure the human body. In addition, breathing compressed air under extreme pressure can have harmful effects.

Scott Carpenter and Bob Barth in Bermuda preparing for first use of Sealab 1 in 1964.

This artist's concept of the Sealab 1 habitat shows it resting on the seabed with divers working on science and engineering tasks close by.

The air surrounding us is about 70 percent nitrogen and 30 percent oxygen. As people descend beneath the surface of the sea, they begin to encounter difficulties with breathing air under pressure. Nitrogen affects the brain, and under pressure it poisons the diver. He or she begins to lose concentration and feel drowsy. Eventually, the diver has such a false sense of well-being that he or she may do something careless, resulting in death. Nitrogen begins to have bad effects at a depth of around 100 feet.

Oxygen poisoning is just as bad. High concentrations of the life-giving gas can intoxicate the brain and cause convulsions. As a diver descends, he or she inhales higher and higher concentrations of oxygen because the air has been compressed. Moreover, when returning to the surface, a diver must slowly exchange the pressure of the surrounding water with the pressure of the atmosphere at sea level. What this means is that divers have to come to the surface very slowly. By doing this they prevent the "bends", caused by too rapid change from high pressure to low pressure.

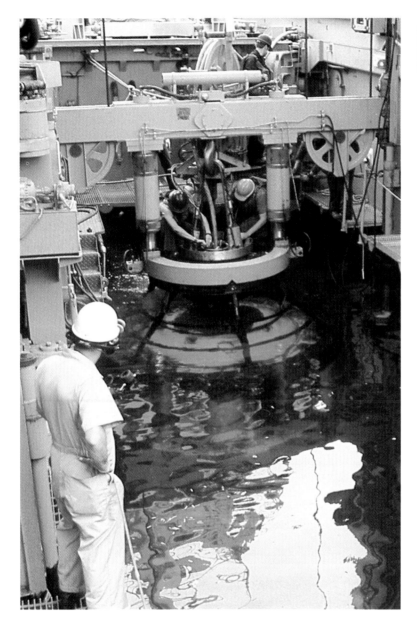

Crewmen of the test-range support ship USS Elk River work on a personnel transfer capsule as it is lowered for a test drive.

When divers get the bends, it means that gas is expanding in the body, forming bubbles that can enter the bloodstream and cause severe pain or even death. Following tests in 1939, the U.S. Navy said that for safety, divers ascending from the maximum allowed diving depth of 380 feet must spend three hours coming to the surface. This slow rise to surface level is called **decompression**. Because of the cold and other dangers, the divers could work at 380 feet for only 30 minutes. Just getting back to the surface took six times as long as their useful work period. The Navy looked for another way of increasing seabed work time and discovered **saturation diving**.

Saturation diving provides the diver with a seabed habitat

pressurized to the outside water pressure. After about a day, the diver's body becomes saturated with the gases in the surrounding air he or she breathes. The diver can go in and out the habitat at will and need go through decompression only once, when returning to the surface after several weeks in the habitat. Sealab was such a habitat, one in which divers could live and work while exploring the bottom of the sea for several weeks at a time.

Sealab was constructed from two floats welded together to form a cigar-shaped cylinder. It was 40 feet long and 10 feet in diameter. Two 12-inch portholes were installed on each side of the chamber. Divers could come and go through two manholes in the bottom of the chamber. **Water ballast** was provided at each end, along with emergency oxygen and electrical equipment. In the middle of the habitat, 24 feet of living space provided bunks, lockers, controls, food containers, a toilet, air-conditioning gear, and storage space for scientific equipment. There were cables going to the surface carrying telephone wires, electrical lines, and compressed air.

Sealab 1 just after completion at the Navy base in Panama City, Florida.

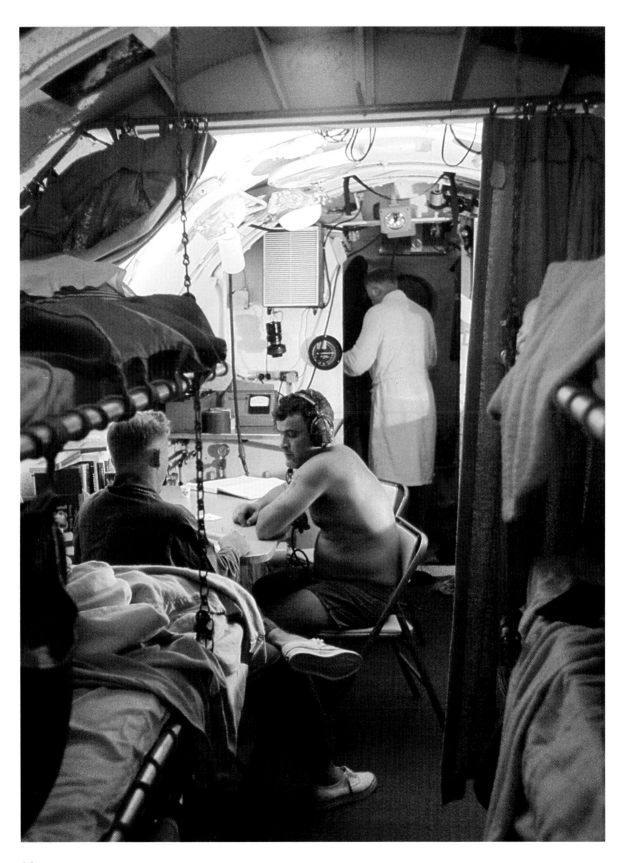

Daily evening routine after dinner aboard Sealab 1 showing the cramped living quarters.

To the Seabed!

Sealab 1 was put into the sea at a site 26 miles off Bermuda. It was linked to a covered **lighter**, or platform, on the surface. The lighter was 260 feet long, 40 feet wide, and equipped to lift large objects. Sealab 1 was lowered near Argus Island, a research platform on stilts. Divers would work with experiments attached to the bottom of Argus Island. The platform had originally been set up to study the use of sound waves in water for mapping objects in the sea. Called **sonar**, this technique builds up a picture-like image of objects underwater.

The site where Sealab 1 was lowered had a reputation for calm seas and good weather. The water was clear and it was fine on the morning of July 19, 1964, when the large object was slowly lowered. It came to rest gently on the bottom, 193 feet beolw the surface. Next day, at 5.30 P.M., four aquanauts moved into Sealab 1 to begin their eleven-day stay. These men had been selected from dozens of volunteers. Malcolm Scott Carpenter was not among them. He would join the aquanauts destined to man the second Sealab scheduled for 1965.

As tests aboard Sealab 1 got under way, divers ventured outside. They would carry out many scientific tests and underwater

Sealab 1 sitting on the bottom of the sea in natural light showing how transparent the water was.

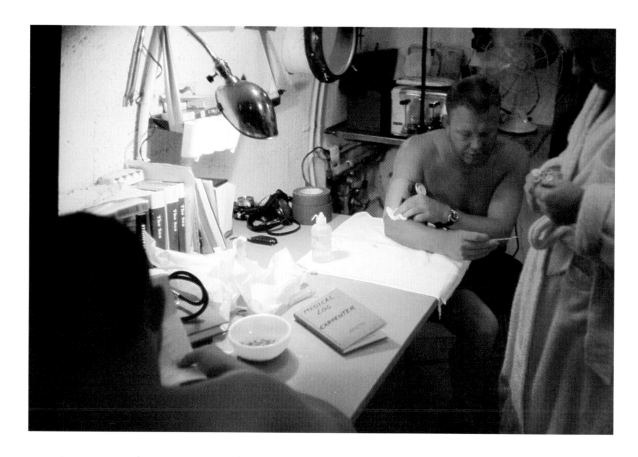

experiments. One diver, Senior Chief Hospital Corpsman Manning was outside taking pictures of a one-man **submersible** practicing a landing on the hatch of a mock submarine. Submersibles are underwater craft capable of carrying people to great depths for short periods. Suddenly, Manning felt light-headed. Recognizing the symptoms of oxygen starvation, he swam back to Sealab 1. Just as he started up the entrance, he lost consciousness and fell back, his tank hitting the side of the lab.

Quick as a flash, Gunner's Mate First Class Lester E. Anderson grabbed Manning's limp body and pulled him inside. Within a minute Manning was breathing again, but blood vessels in his eyes had ruptured, turning them first red and then black. The third aquanaut, Dr. Robert E. Thompson, gave him a thorough check and found no permanent damage. Manning was allowed to stay and continue his work with Anderson, Thompson, and the fourth aquanaut, veteran Genesis crewman, Chief Quartermaster Bob Barth.

As the days went by the aquanauts settled into their routine and Thompson kept a diary of events: "Up at about 07:00 to assist Bob who complains of mild aching joints; others and myself also have the same complaint. I took a short swim outside in only my swimsuit and

Each day aboard Sealab 1, crew members took blood samples for special medical tests.

weight belt. It was chilly at first, but soon felt good and quite refreshing. There seem to be many fish and other varieties of sea life." Each day a small **pressure chamber** carrying newspapers, magazines, and food was lowered to Sealab 1 for the four aquanauts. They were proving that humans could live on the seabed and do useful work.

Toward the end of their eleven days in Sealab 1, the aquanauts gave thanks for their wonderful achievement, as told by Thompson's diary: "26 July, 1964. 10:30 — Church service, very simple, very brief. I noted our feelings of thankfulness for our safe descent and good care while we have been here. I tried to play "Onward Christian Soldiers" on my harmonica but seemed to choke up a bit today." The four men returned to the surface during the morning of July 31. What they had done would pave the way for a more ambitious test, one that would involve the second NASA astronaut to orbit the earth.

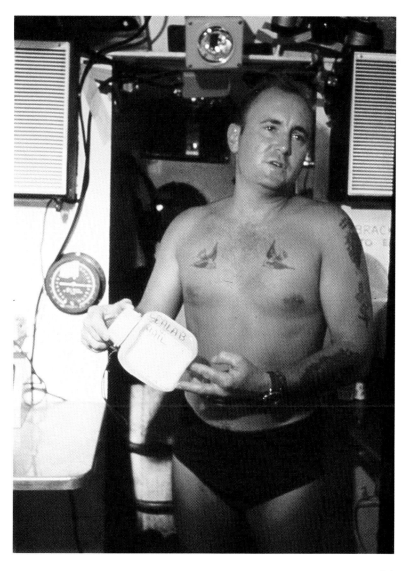

A crushed plastic bottle sent down with the mail failed to resist the pressure of air inside the habitat.

An aerial close-up of Sealab 2 in the water with divers working around the deck.

From Astronaut to Aquanaut

Sealab 1 had been pressurized with 80 percent nitrogen, and 4 percent oxygen. The human body does not need a lot of oxygen and, to reduce the amount of nitrogen, helium was substituted instead of nitrogen. About the only noticeable effect is that helium gives the human voice a squeaky sound. Even the deepest voice ends up sounding like Donald Duck! The mixed gas atmosphere was pressurized at a staggering 86 pounds per square inch, the same as the water pressure 193 feet beneath the surface. The earth's atmosphere at sea level is just 14.7 pounds per square inch.

Sealab 2 was to be different from the first lab. To begin with, it was built with a specific purpose in mind. Whereas Sealab 1 had been made from used floats, the second lab was built for the job. It looked like a railroad tank car without wheels and had a small **conning tower**, or raised cylindrical structure on top. Sealab 2 was 57 feet long and 12 feet in diameter and had a cement floor for ballast. Outside, it had a protective anti-shark cage around the conning tower and 24 gas bottles. Inside, the atmosphere would be similar to that provided for Sealab 1.

Malcolm Scott Carpenter had been loaned by NASA to head the first two teams of aquanauts scheduled to visit Sealab 2. He would remain at the bottom of the sea while his nine colleagues in the first team returned to the surface after fifteen days. He would head up the second team of nine additional aquanauts for a further fifteen days and then return to the surface. In all, Carpenter would spend more than four weeks on the seabed.

The visit began on the morning of August 28, 1965, when the first ten divers put on their scuba gear and plunged over the side of their ship to swim down to Sealab 2. Two days earlier the habitat had been gently lowered to the sea floor at a depth of 205 feet, within sight of La Jolla, California. The site was very different to that used in Sealab 1. It was dark, cold, and more typical of places Navy divers would have to work on future tasks. Very soon, the ten men were on board Sealab 2 and about to make a historic telephone link-up with two orbiting astronauts in space.

As the second American to orbit the earth, Carpenter had a special interest in talking with astronauts Cooper and Conrad in Gemini 5. He commented to them that swimming around outside his capsule

A Sealab 2 diver trains with a porpoise prior to the project's underwater experiment.

was easier for him than for the two spacemen! Life aboard Sealab 2 was hectic, and there was little time for rest. His two astronaut companions in space were resting for long periods as part of their mission to prove that two men could remain in space for eight days, about the time required to get to the moon and return. Below the sea, the ten aquanauts carried out numerous tests. They erected platforms on the sea floor, tried out various tools, set up fish cages and TV cameras, and performed scientific experiments.

At one point they talked with French marine explorer Jacques Cousteau several thousand miles away in his habitat Conshelf 3 on the floors of the Mediterranean Sea. Communication was difficult. The squeaky voices could not easily be heard, and instructions from the surface were easily misunderstood. There was too little time for rest, and the aquanauts learned a lot about how to work out proper schedules and routines. As Carpenter testified, "the days on the bottom often consisted of 20 hours of steady work." It went quickly because of that, however, and Sealab 2 performed its first exchange of crews on September 12, 1965. While Carpenter stayed aboard, his nine colleagues returned to the surface and another nine men swam to the habitat. Like their predecessors, they would stay down for fifteen days.

Every day mail and items requested by the crew were lowered from the surface to Sealab 2.

Working inside the cramped quarters of Sealab 2 was always difficult.

Life aboard Sealab 2

During the exchange of divers at the end of fifteen days aboard Sealab 2, Carpenter was stung on the arm by a scorpion fish. This caused his arm to swell to several times its normal size and provided a useful opportunity to test the effect of drugs in the highly pressurized, helium-rich atmosphere. His arm recovered within 24 hours.

Life on Sealab 2 was very different from life at the surface. The helium atmosphere almost destroyed any sense of smell, and at one point the crew was threatened by burned toast filling the lab with poisonous odors nobody could smell. And it was no easier trying to enjoy a cup of coffee. Helium quickly disperses heat, even in a coffee cup. Within seconds a steaming mug of coffee cooled off, as though it had been left out in the cold.

Cooking was a real problem that could become a serious danger. Griddle cakes would burn on the underside, yet remain uncooked on top. Because the coils of the electric stove would never glow red,

Scene from inside Sealab, a grouper noses around the porthole.

Sealab 3 was to have been more ambitious than Sealab 2 and would have operated from greater depth than earlier Sealab habitats.

there was no way of knowing which burners were hot and which were cold. Very soon, burned hands and fingers sent crew members rushing for the medical kit. It was an unpleasant way to discover which burner had been turned on.

It was very difficult bringing a kettle of water to a boil. In the strange underwater world, water refused to boil below 328 degrees and would quickly cool off. When the divers baked a cake and removed it from its container, it promptly collapsed. Putting it aside and thinking it was ruined, the crew rushed back to eat it when several hours it suddenly rose to perfection. The scientists were hard put to find an answer.

The crew got used to catching local food like **plankton** floating past the lab. They trained a porpoise they called Tuffy to recognize sounds. Soon, Tuffy was scurrying back and forth between Sealab and the surface taking messages and returning with mail. From their underwater habitat, Carpenter and his nine colleagues provided much valuable information on how divers could work for long hours using electrically heated wet suits, new equipment for underwater rescue, and special techniques for marine research.

When Carpenter returned to the surface after spending 30 days more than 200 feet down, he brought a wealth of scientific information. With two separate teams of brave, pioneering explorers, he had opened up a new world. It was as though the man from outer space was pointing mankind toward a new, exciting world of inner space. A third group of ten men spent another fifteen-day period on the bottom, and the Sealab 2 visits ended when they came to the surface on October 10, 1965.

Carpenter was involved in planning longer expeditions to deeper locations. Sealab 3 was designed to sit about 600 feet below the surface, where the pressure of the atmosphere inside would have to be an incredible 265 pounds per square inch to equal the pressure of the water outside the lab. The project was delayed, and not until February 1969 was Sealab 3 lowered to the ocean floor near San Clemente Island, off the California coast. It sprang a leak, and while divers tried to repair it, one of them collapsed and died. The project was cancelled. It was the end of a great adventure.

Aquanauts work to attach lines from the USS Elk River to the Sealab 3 habitat.

A workman directs the crane operator as a personnel transfer capsule is lowered in to position aboard the USS Elk River.

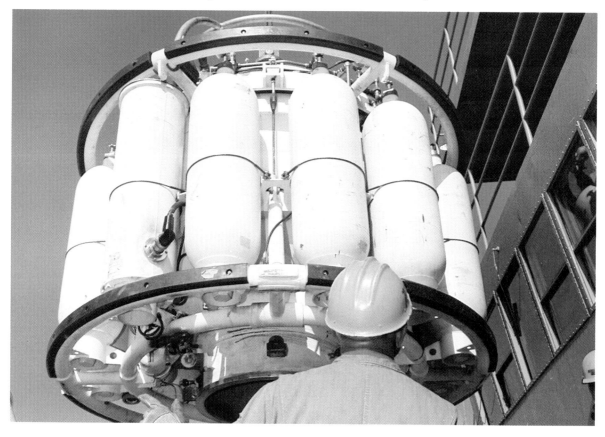

Glossary

Bends, the

The painful and often fatal damage caused to divers by bubbles in their bodies when they return to the surface too quickly after deep dives.

Conning tower

Raised cylindrical tower found on the deck of submarines and other underwater vessels.

Decompression

What a diver has to go through after being underwater for a period of time to prevent the bends. The pressure is reduced slowly, usually in a decompression chamber.

Heat shield

Shield to protect space capsule and stop it from burning up on its reentry into the earth's atmosphere.

Lighter

Large, flat-bottomed platform or barge used for on and off loading ships.

Orbit

A circular path traveled around a planet or star.

Plankton

Minute organisms found in the ocean.

Pressure chamber

Small vehicle pressurized to the same air pressure as the water pressure outside.

Saturation diving

Deep diving in which the diver's body becomes saturated, enabling the diver to stay at depth for many hours, or even days.

Scuba

Self-contained underwater breathing apparatus, used for breathing while swimming underwater.

Sonar

Equipment that can "see" through water in the dark by using sound rays instead of light rays.

Submersible

A vehicle, like a submarine, that carries people underwater and protects them from the pressure of the water outside.

Underwater habitats

Places where scientists and engineers can work and live for weeks at a time.

Water ballast

Water used to fill ballast tanks in a vessel to give it weight and stability.

FROM SPACE TO
SEABED

Index